Anomaly Flats
A to Z

Written by Clayton Smith
Illustrated by Steven Luna

Dapper Press

To Maple, who came into this world fearless, and curious.
This is for you. - *C.S.*

To Alex, Lijy, and Zane, for the weird, magical little world
we inhabit together. - *S.L.*

You're about to enter an alien realm,
Anomaly Flats, as it's known,
lies at the end of a spiraling road,
in a dimension all its own.

The oddest folks you'll surely encounter,
the strangest sights you'll see.
Come with us now as we present the town
of Anomaly Flats, A to Z.

A

is for the Abberations,
our ghostly baseball
team,

B is for Farmer Buchheit, whose cows aren't what they seem.

C is for the evil twin who creeps out of Clone Lake,

E

is for eggs,
which are extremely
against the law,

F is for the festering flies that swarm from Marcy's jaw.

G is for the ghastly green glow that ruined old man Seymour's day.

H

is for old Hillcrest Manor,
home of the haunted
soirée.

I

is for interdimensional travel that takes you through a worm hole,

J

is for the Jansport backpack
that holds all the things
you stole.

K is for killer rabbits –
oh no, they escaped from
the zoo!

L is for lurkers in the Lurchwood Forest...I wouldn't camp here if I were you.

N is for the Nite-Owl Diner – today's special is tentacle soup!

O

is for the ogle-brained
Oracle, telling fortunes
as she skates,

P is for peculiar Plasma Creek, which can alter your physical states,

Q is for questions, and there are so many...what's going on in Anomaly Flats?

R

is for the runes in the
Roach Motel that protect you
from demons and bats,

S is for strange Anomaly Flats science...Lewis says, "Knowledge is power!"

T is for time capsule, a terrible tomb, and boy, it sure does smell sour.

V is for the vexing Void in the night, with its vibrating discontents.

W is for that one wild, wicked walk in Walmart... don't go down Aisle 8!

X

is for Lewis' leaky canister,
his weirdest concoction
to date.

FORMULA

X.

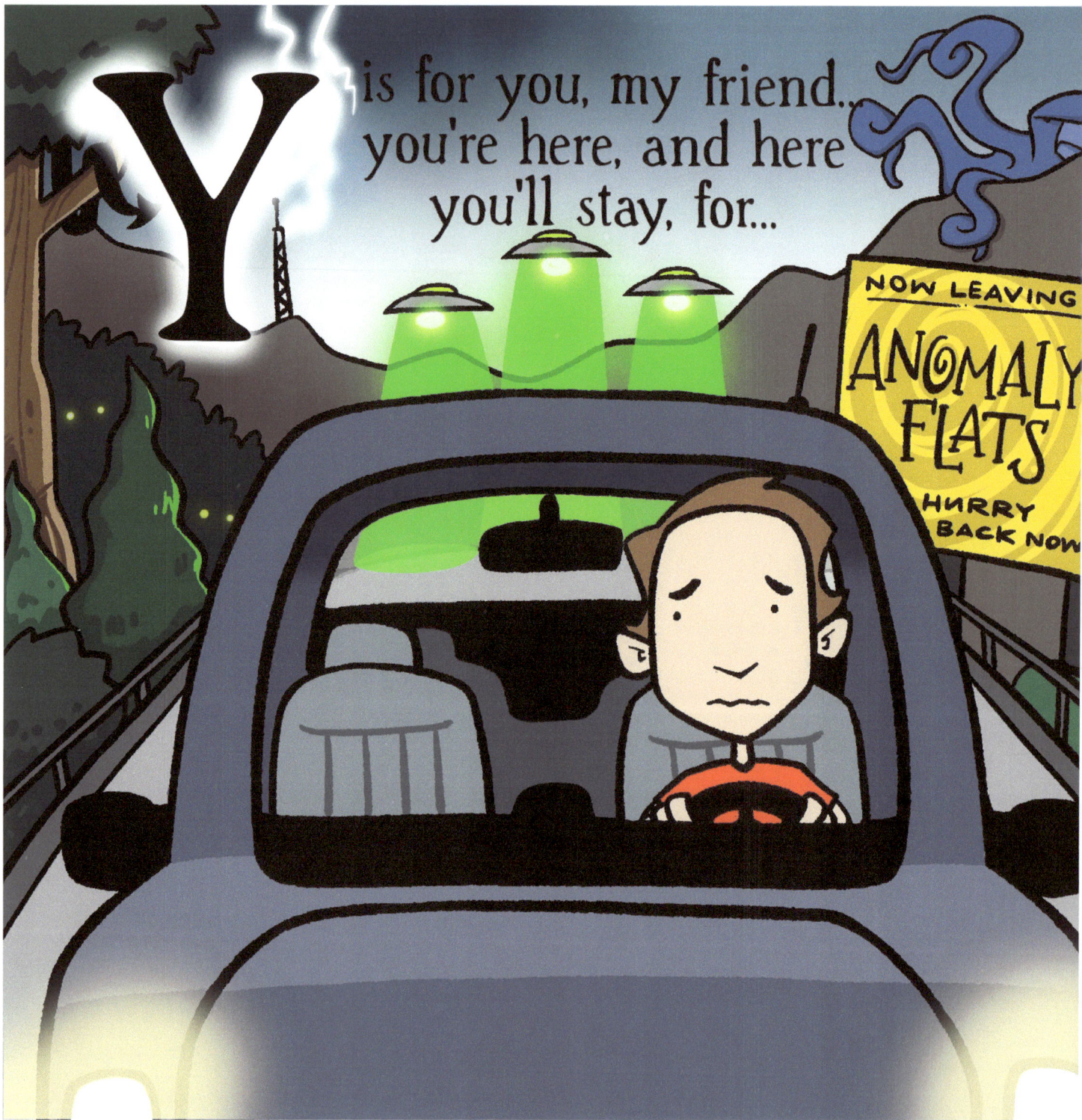

Z is the zig-zag path that will bring you back to us as it leads you away.

About the Creators

Clayton Smith lives in Anomaly Flats. Would you please come get him?

Steven Luna is not an alien... at least not that he knows.